Irresistible Fondues

> Author: **Angelika Ilies** | Photos: **Jörn Rynio**

Contents

Fundamentals

The Recipes

Appendix

Fondue—Fresh, Fast, and Fun

Serving fondue is an easy and enjoyable way to entertain your friends in a relaxed, social atmosphere. It lets you prepare all the ingredients at your leisure and then enjoy the entire meal with your guests. Everything is done right at the table and your guests all participate in cooking their own food.

Colorful skewers and fancy meatballs, fresh vegetables, rich meats, and delicate seafood—you'll find all the ingredients that go into this fondue to be appetite-pleasing.

Fondue Basics

1 | Space Requirements

There has to be enough room at the table to cook your fondue without any undue risk. The pot sizzling in the center reaches very high temperatures, so you'll want to maintain a little distance.

No more than six people should dine from a fondue pot at one time. If there are more, they'll have difficulty accessing the pot, and the large quantities of food dipped in the oil or stock will cool it down too much. If you are expecting eight to ten people, borrow a second pot from a friend.

1
Supplement homemade dips and sauces with prepared products.

2 | Which Fondue is For You?

Fondue cooked in hot oil in a pot makes food wonderfully crispy but can be a little too rich for some people. Simmering stock is a gentler way to cook meat, fish, and vegetables, and results in a finished meal that is lighter but equally as delicious. Another choice is cheese fondue, which wraps ingredients in a rich, buttery coating and is pleasantly tangy.

3 | Variety is Key!

When choosing a fondue, consider both taste and time involved to prepare everything. Don't be afraid to take advantage of some of the excellent prepared products on the market to save time, for example, pairing puréed garlic from a jar with fresh herbs, a little wine, and mascarpone to make a delicious sauce.

4 | Quantities

The classic fondue recipes in this book (accompanied by dips, sauces, and other side

2 *Since there's no risk of overcooking anything, feel free to enjoy a cocktail with your guests.*

dishes) are designed for four people. Use half a recipe if you make fondue for two. For six, prepare one of the variations mentioned as well. Experience has shown that 5 to $8\frac{1}{2}$ oz of meat or fish are required per person, or less if you offer a wide selection of vegetables and/or fruit.

5 | Pure Relaxation

A lot of the preparation for a fondue can be done ahead of time if you keep the ingredients tightly sealed in the refrigerator until right before the dinner begins. Then when you're ready to eat, it's a snap to bring the food to the table.

Pots & Plates

To enjoy fondue, you must have a suitable pot that can be heated at the table. Such pots are available in various shapes and are made of different materials—ask for recommendations at a kitchen specialty store. And be sure to save the operating instructions as a reference. Provide each guest with a special fondue plate or a regular dinner plate, ideally accompanied by a knife and fork for dining, and fondue fork for cooking. If you use an Asian hot pot, impress your guests by offering rice bowls, chopsticks in place of traditional cutlery, and long-handled wire ladles.

Classic

A stainless steel or enameled fondue pot usually comes with a burner that holds the pot securely in place. It's also nice to have a metal lid on the pot that prevents splattering and is designed to support the fondue forks.

Safe

If you choose to use an electric fondue pot, be sure to fasten the power cord securely to the table.

Asian

For authentic Asian fondue, you need a special "hot pot" with a funnel-shaped chimney in the middle. You can, however, get by with a classic fondue pot. The important thing is that the burner be hot enough.

Cheese Fondue Pot

"Caquelons" are the wide, glazed clay or earthenware pots typically used for cheese fondue. They never get too hot and transfer the heat evenly to the cheese.

Oil Fondue—When You Want It Crispy

1 | Here's How

With an oil fondue, everything is cooked at the table in some type of high-heat cooking oil or fat. Your guests spear the prepared, bite-size ingredients with fondue forks, fry them in the hot oil, dunk them in a dip, and enjoy them. In the case of the classic bourguignonne fondue, only beef filet is cooked. If you find this too boring, there are many alternatives, including those found on pages 25–31.

2 | Basics

➤ Fill the pot only halfway with oil. Otherwise it might splatter during the meal and catch fire on the lit burner. Always be aware of this fire hazard.

1 Bite-size ingredients are cooked in the hot oil on fondue forks.

➤ First heat the oil in the fondue pot on the stove until it instantly turns a bread cube golden brown. Then carefully transfer the pot to the table and set it on top of the lit burner.

➤ You'll also need to keep the oil hot at the table; if the oil isn't hot enough the ingredients will soak up too much of the oil. So be careful not to put too many ingredients into the pot at one time to avoid cooling down the oil. And take occasional breaks to let the oil heat up again.

➤ After frying the food in oil, let it drain for a moment on the edge of the pot to remove some of the grease.

➤ Place the cooked ingredients on a plate and let them cool slightly before eating.

➤ Rather than the fondue fork, which could burn your lips and tongue as it comes out of the hot oil, use a regular fork to gobble up these tasty morsels.

2 Heat the oil on the stove top before bringing it to the table.

3 | The Pot

The pot must fit exactly into the burner stand to give it stability. A special fondue pot is preferable, but you can also use a standard stainless steel or enameled pot if you have a suitable burner, or else set the pot on an electric hotplate. It's best to use a pot that narrows at the top in order to prevent the oil from splattering. A metal lid with notches can be set on top, both to keep the oil from splashing out and to hold the forks in place.

Ingredients for Oil Fondues

l: Fill the fondue pot
h a pure vegetable
or a solid vegetable
ortening with a high
oke point. These
s can be heated
a sufficiently high
nperature without
rning or splattering.
ver use butter
margarine since
y will burn before
coming hot enough.

Meat: The traditional
meat for oil fondue is
filet of beef but you can
also cook any other kind
of meat. The best meats
are pieces of beef, veal,
pork, lamb, chicken,
and turkey. But you can
also cook bratwurst,
spareribs, small cutlets,
any of the ingredients
on pages 25–31, and
much more.

Fish: Any firm fish fillet
that is suitable for
skewers can be pre-
pared in an oil fondue.
Examples of good
choices are cod, salmon,
tuna, and monkfish.

Vegetables: In addi-
tion to meat and fish,
you can cook all kinds
of vegetables. Basically,
any vegetable that
tastes good raw or fries
quickly is suitable for
fondue (also see recipes
starting on page 25).
Vegetables with longer
cooking times, such as
green beans, should
be precooked.

Basic Recipe

Melting Away
The original fondue from Switzerland, which gives its name to all other types of fondue known today, was made with melted cheese. The term itself comes from the French word "fonder," meaning, "to melt." Once upon a time, it was simply a way to eat leftovers. Mountain peasants melted dried out cheese in wine and dipped cubes of bread into it.

Cheese Fondue

SERVES 4:
- ➤ 1¹⁄₄ lb Gruyère
- 1¹⁄₂ cups dry white wine
- 3 tsp cornstarch
- 6 tbs kirsch
- Pepper
- Freshly grated nutmeg
- Loaf of bread (approx 1 lb), cut into cubes

TIP

Types of Cheese
Gruyère and Emmenthaler are two traditional fondue cheeses. Use either one type alone or mix them together, as in the case of the Swiss Cheese Fondue (see page 21).

1 *Dice the cheese finely or grate it coarsely using a food processor or a standard grater.*

2 *In the caquelon, gently heat wine on the stove. Gradually add and melt cheese while stirring constantly.*

3 *Stir cornstarch into kirsch until smooth. Add to cheese while stirring, bring to a boil, and season with pepper and nutmeg.*

4 *Place caquelon on burner to keep it h Spear bread cube fondue forks and them around in th cheese mixture.*

Troubleshooting

Cheese won't melt

➤ Dice cheese finely or grate coarsely and slowly melt it into wine that is not too hot while stirring constantly. If you want to try out a new type of cheese, test it first to see if it melts in wine and yields a creamy mixture.

Cheese and wine won't merge

➤ Always use a wooden spoon and stir in a figure-eight pattern. If that doesn't help, the wine is probably not acidic enough, so add a little lemon juice. Remember to use acidic, dry white wine such as a Sauvignon Blanc or Chenin Blanc.

Cheese mixture is too thick

➤ Gradually stir in a little wine to thin the fondue.

Cheese mixture is too runny

➤ Add a little more cheese or thicken the wine-cheese mixture with a little cornstarch stirred into kirsch.

Cheese and wine have separated

➤ Even during the meal, you have to stir the cheese mixture constantly to keep it nice and creamy. If that isn't enough, return the pot to the stove, reheat the fondue, and add a little lemon juice while stirring vigorously.

Burned onto the bottom

➤ If the heat was too high, turn it down immediately. If necessary, pour the cheese mixture into another pot, clean the fondue pot, pour the cheese mixture back into it, and lower the burner flame.

Cheese mixture tastes bland

➤ The cheese didn't have enough flavor. Season the mixture with spices or herbs, such as freshly ground pepper, chives, dill, curry powder, or try adding reconstituted dried mushrooms.

Bread in the cheese

➤ Every cube of bread should have a little crust on it so it spears better and doesn't fall off the fondue fork. Don't use bread that's too light and airy.

Guests are full too quickly

➤ Fondue, especially classic cheese fondue, can become filling very fast. Besides bread, try dipping lighter items such as mushrooms, shrimp, zucchini slices, and broccoli into the cheese.

Light Fondues: Hot Pots

1 | Here's How

These fondues originated in Asia and are as much a part of Asian tradition as cheese fondue is to Switzerland. As a light, low-calorie alternative to oil fondues, hot pots are currently very popular. A seasoned stock or water is simmered and diners dunk their choice of ingredients into the pot using a wire ladle, a fondue fork, or chopsticks. Or you can simply place various ingredients in the pot, let them cook for several minutes, and fish them out with a ladle.

2 | Basics

➤ Prepare all the ingredients ahead of time by cutting

1 Ingredients are held in the stock in special ladles.

them into small pieces or thin slices.

➤ For the stock, feel free to use prepared products. Don't stir too vigorously. The stock becomes tangier as it cooks.

➤ Bring at least 3–4 quarts stock to a boil in a pot on the stove. Over the course of a long fondue meal, the liquid in the hot pot boils away and needs constant replenishing.

➤ Fill the hot pot or fondue pot halfway with boiling stock and place on top of the lit burner on the table.

➤ The stock must be bubbling if the food is to become crispy, juicy, and flavorful. Don't put too many ingredients in the stock at one time and take a break once in a while so the stock can return to a boil.

➤ Hold the ingredients in the stock with a skewer or ladle and then eat it off your plate with chopsticks or a fork.

➤ As the food cooks, the hot stock takes on a wonderful

2 Cut all ingredients into small pieces so they'll cook quickly in the stock.

flavor and can be served at the end of the meal (or the next day) as soup.

3 | The Pot

The Mongolian hot pot with the funnel-shaped chimney in the middle is typically used, but you can also place a standard fondue pot or a nice stainless steel pot on the table. The important thing is to have a large burner that produces enough heat. To be absolutely safe, heat the pot on a single-burner electric hotplate.

Ingredients for Asian Fondues

ock: The base for
an fondue is a meat,
ultry, fish, or veg-
ble stock that is not
hearty. Feel free to
prepared stock but
ou have the time
d energy, it's best to
ke your own. To give
he right flavor, add
ttle ginger, garlic,
rry, star anise, soy
uce, rice wine, cori-
der, or other common
an seasonings.

Meat & Fish: Anything
is suitable that can be
cooked in hot stock in
just a few minutes and
turns out tender. Lamb
is traditional for the
Mongolian hot pot but
you can also cook filet of
beef, pork, veal, chicken,
turkey, and fish. Cut the
meat into thin slices
rather than cubes so it
will cook more quickly
in the hot stock.

Vegetables: Almost
any vegetable goes with
Asian fondue. Tender
types such as bean
sprouts, green onions,
Chinese cabbage, or
zucchini can be set out
raw. Firmer vegetables
like cauliflower, carrots,
and sugar snap peas
must be blanched briefly
beforehand.

Other Ingredients:
You can make anything
available at the table
that cooks quickly or
can be heated up in hot
stock, including the
delicacies on pages 33
to 39. Typical ingredi-
ents for Asian fondues
include glass noodles,
cooked rice, and mari-
nated tofu.

Classic Fondues

What would a fondue cookbook be without the classics, including Fondue Bourguignonne, Mongolian Hot Pot, and Cheese Fondue? Here they are, along with other traditional fondue favorites. All the recipes are designed for four people, so you can either follow them exactly or derive your own creations by mixing and matching them with the many ideas presented on pages 25–39.

Quick Recipes

Fondue Bourguignonne

SERVES 4:

➤ 1³/₄ lb beef filet | Oil for frying

1 | Remove gristle and excess fat from meat, cut into bite-size cubes, and arrange on a platter.

2 | Heat oil in the fondue pot on the stove, transfer to the lit burner, and keep hot. Serve with white bread or a baguette and with salt and pepper. For dips and side dishes, see page 58.

Rustic Fondue

SERVES 4:

➤ 1¹/₃ lb Swiss cheese | 5 thin slices bacon, cut into small cubes (approx 3¹/₂ oz) | 1¹/₂ cups wine | 2 tbs lemon juice | 3 tsp cornstarch | 4 tbs Calvados | Pepper | Nutmeg | Loaf of bread (approx 1 lb), cut into cubes

1 | Grate cheese coarsely. Fry bacon in fondue pot until golden brown. Pour in wine and lemon juice and heat.

2 | Melt cheese in pot while stirring constantly. Stir cornstarch into Calvados until smooth and add. Bring to a boil while stirring and season with pepper and nutmeg. Place on the lit burner and keep hot. Serve with bread cubes and side dishes on page 21.

13

Fast | Inexpensive

Mixed Meat and Vegetable Fondue

SERVES 4:

➤ 1 red bell pepper

2 small zucchini

7 oz shiitake mushrooms (may substitute cremini mushrooms)

1$\frac{1}{3}$ lb mixed meat (e.g., beef, pork, veal, lamb, turkey, chicken)

Oil for frying

🕐 Prep time: 30 minutes

➤ Calories per serving: About 455

1 | Rinse bell pepper and zucchini, trim, and cut into bite-size pieces. Rinse mushrooms and remove stems.

2 | Rinse meat under cold water, pat dry, and cut into bite-size cubes. Arrange all ingredients on platters or plates.

3 | Heat oil on the stove in the fondue pot. Transfer to the lit burner and keep hot.

4 | At the table, spear the desired ingredients with fondue forks and cook in hot oil.

TIPS

Other ingredients to try:

➤ Any vegetable that can be cooked in hot oil when raw or after brief par-boiling.

➤ Little sausages such as spicy Spanish chorizos or Vienna sausages.

➤ As an addition to classic fondue, try some fancy recipes to cook in your fondue pot such as satay skewers, vegetable rolls, or chicken wings (see starting on page 25).

1 Prepare
Cut vegetables and meat into bite-size pieces.

2 Heat
Heat oil in the fondue pot on the stove.

3 At the table
Spear ingredients with fondue forks and simmer in the hot oil.

15

Specialty of China | Hearty
Mongolian Hot Pot

SERVES 4:
- 3^1/$_2$ oz glass noodles

  3^1/$_2$ oz Chinese egg noodles

  1^1/$_3$ lean lamb (e.g., from saddle or leg)

  1 medium head Chinese cabbage (about 1^1/$_2$ lb)

  5 oz leafy Chinese vegetables (e.g., bok choy)

  7 oz tofu

  3 quarts mild chicken stock

  1 piece fresh ginger (walnut-size)

⏱ Prep time: 40 minutes
- Calories per serving: About 840

1 | Pour hot water over glass noodles and soak for 15 minutes. Cook egg noodles in boiling water according to package directions, then pour into a colander and drain.

2 | Rinse meat, pat dry, remove gristle and excess fat, and cut into paper-thin slices.

3 | Trim Chinese cabbage and leafy vegetables, rinse, and cut into strips ¾ inch–1¼ inch wide. Slice tofu. Drain glass noodles and cut up with scissors if desired. Decoratively arrange all ingredients on plates or platters.

4 | Heat stock on the stove in a pot. Fill hot pot at least halfway with hot stock and keep remaining stock on the kitchen stove over low heat.

5 | Peel ginger and add to hot pot. Keep the stock in the hot pot simmering on the table.

6 | At the table, hold ingredients in the stock using fondue ladles or chopsticks and cook. Or place ingredients in the simmering stock and then fish out with ladles. Season with various sauces. Occasionally add more hot stock to the hot pot. Afterwards (or the next day), season stock to taste with leftover sauces or a little rice wine and serve as soup.

- Serve with: Soy sauce, chili sauce, hoisin sauce, or one of the sauces in this book (starting on page 41).

TIPS

Best with lamb
- This fondue is traditionally prepared with lamb and various vegetables, but other types of meat, seafood, and fish are also excellent.
- If desired, place meat in the freezer for 20–30 minutes so it will be easier to cut into paper-thin slices.

Specialty of Japan

Shrimp and Vegetable Tempura

SERVES 4:

➤ 8 oz raw peeled shrimp
  7 oz shiitake mushrooms
  1¾ lb mixed vegetables (green beans, broccoli, cauliflower, eggplant, zucchini)
  1 cup plus 1 tbs flour
  Oil for frying
  2 egg yolks
  ½ tsp salt

🕐 Prep time: 45 minutes
➤ Calories per serving: About 755

1 | Rinse shrimp under cold water and dry. Wipe off mushrooms with a damp cloth and remove stems. Rinse vegetables, clean, and cut into bite-size pieces. Precook each vegetable individually in boiling water until just barely al dente. Remove, rinse in ice-cold water, and drain.

2 | Dust shrimp, mushrooms, and vegetables with a thin coating of flour. Shake off excess and arrange on platters.

3 | Heat oil in the fondue pot on the stove. Transfer to the lit burner and keep hot.

4 | Just before serving, stir together egg yolks, 1 cup ice-cold water, remaining flour, and salt until smooth. Serve batter in individual bowls.

5 | At the table, spear ingredients with fondue forks, dip into batter, let excess drip off, and cook in hot oil.

➤ Accompaniments: Soy sauce, wasabi, Asian sauces, and dips

Specialty of Japan

Shabu Shabu

SERVES 4:

➤ 3 oz glass noodles
  1⅓ lb beef filet
  7 oz tofu
  1 bunch green onions
  1 large carrot
  3½ oz shiitake mushrooms
  3½ oz spinach leaves (may substitute watercress)
  1 small head Chinese cabbage
  1 piece kombu (type of seaweed; may substitute nori or other seaweed)

🕐 Prep time: 30 minutes
➤ Calories per serving: About 375

1 | Pour hot water over glass noodles and soak for 15 minutes. Rinse meat under cold water, pat dry, and cut into paper-thin slices. Cut tofu into small pieces.

2 | Rinse and clean vegetables. Cut green onions into thin strips. Peel carrot and cut into small pieces. Wipe shiitakes and remove stems. Sort spinach. Cut Chinese cabbage into narrow strips. Drain glass noodles. Arrange all ingredients on platters.

3 | Bring about 3 quarts water to a boil on the stove and simmer seaweed for 10 minutes. Remove seaweed and pour a sufficient amount of water into the hot pot. Transfer to the burner and simmer while keeping remaining water hot.

4 | At the table, cook ingredients in the stock and fish them out using fondue ladles or chopsticks, occasionally adding hot stock. Afterwards, serve the stock as soup.

Specialty of Switzerland | Vegetarian

Swiss Cheese Fondue

SERVES 4:

- 1 clove garlic
  10^1/$_2$ oz each of Gruyère and Emmenthaler
  Loaf of bread (approx 1 lb)
  1^1/$_2$ cups dry white wine (e.g., Sauvignon Blanc)
  3 tsp cornstarch
  4 tbs kirsch
  Pepper
  Nutmeg
  A little lemon juice

- Prep time: 40 minutes
- Calories per serving: About 985

1 | Peel garlic, cut in half, and rub around the inside of the caquelon.

2 | Dice cheese finely or grate. Cut bread into bite-size cubes and serve in a basket.

3 | Slowly heat wine in the caquelon on the stove. Gradually add cheese while stirring constantly with a mixing spoon in a figure-eight pattern. First melt cheese over low heat and then bring to a boil.

4 | Stir cornstarch into kirsch until smooth, add to cheese, and bring to a boil. Season with pepper and nutmeg. Continue stirring until all ingredients have blended together in a smooth mixture, adding a little lemon juice if necessary. Transfer cheese fondue to the burner and keep warm over a low flame.

5 | At the table, spear bread cubes with fondue forks and stir around in the cheese mixture.

TIP If anything goes wrong, turn to the troubleshooting tips for cheese fondue on page 9.

- Variation: For a spicy flavor, simply stir 2 fresh, very finely chopped chili peppers or ^{1}/$_2$ tsp dried, crumbled chili pepper into the cheese mixture. For a fondue with Irish beer, finely dice 1^1/$_3$ lb Cheddar. In the caquelon, heat 1 cup Guinness and very gradually add cheese while stirring constantly. Stir 2 tsp cornstarch into a little whiskey until smooth and use to bind cheese mixture. Season with pepper and serve with dark rustic bread and small boiled potatoes.

- Serve with: Mixed pickles and gherkins; various types of bread and rolls; fruits such as pears, bananas, or apples; vegetables with short cooking times such as mushrooms or zucchini; small cooked potatoes; baby corn, either marinated in a jar or blanched; cooked, peeled shrimp; small cubes of cooked ham or cooked chicken breast.

Specialty of
Switzerland

Geneva Cheese Fondue

SERVES 4:

- Loaf of bread (approx 1 lb), or mixed loaves

  3$\frac{1}{2}$ tbs butter

  12 oz Emmenthaler

  8 egg yolks

  White pepper

  Freshly grated nutmeg

  Salt

  $\frac{1}{2}$ cup heavy cream

  2 tbs dry white wine or lemon juice

🕐 Prep time: 45 minutes
- Calories per serving: About 1320

1 | Cut bread into bite-size cubes. In a wide pan, melt 3 tbs butter, toast bread cubes until golden brown, and set aside.

2 | Grate cheese finely. In the caquelon, stir together cheese, egg yolks, and a little pepper, nutmeg, and salt. Stir constantly over low heat. Gradually add remaining butter in bits while stirring vigorously. Do not let the mixture boil.

3 | When the cheese mixture has thickened, stir in cream and wine or lemon juice. Keep hot on the lit burner but don't let it boil. Serve with bread.

- Serve with: Pickles, capers, cocktail onions, and marinated baby corn.

TIP Don't let the cheese mixture boil because this will cause the egg yolk to curdle. If this does happen, immediately stir in a little lemon juice.

Specialty of Italy

Fonduta

SERVES 4:

- 10 oz fontina (Italian raw-milk cheese)

  1 cup milk

  3 tbs butter

  3 egg yolks

  White pepper

  1 lb loaf Italian bread

  1 white truffle

🕐 Prep time: 45 minutes
🕐 Soaking time: 6 hours
- Calories per serving: About 820

1 | Remove rind from cheese and dice very finely. Pour milk over the top, cover, and soak for 6 hours (or overnight).

2 | Place cheese and milk in a hot double boiler and melt cheese over low heat while stirring constantly. Add butter and melt.

3 | In a cup, whisk together a little of the cheese mixture with the egg yolks and add this mixture back into the remaining cheese while stirring. Continue stirring until the mixture is smooth. Season with pepper.

4 | Cut bread into bite-size cubes. Gently wipe off truffle and cut into paper-thin slices. Pour cheese mixture into individual, pre-warmed bowls and serve with bread and truffle.

- Serve with: Finely sliced mushrooms and cherry tomatoes.

Photo top: **Geneva Cheese Fondue**   *Photo bottom:* **Fonduta** ➤

Exotic Oil Fondues

Do you think Asian satay skewers, crunchy spring rolls, and crispy chicken wings are more exciting than the same old beef and pork fillet? Then instead of all meat fondue, try some of these delicacies. The recipes in this chapter not only provide some variety but will also convince any skeptics that fondue can be a lot of fun. Just thread everything onto skewers, hold it in the hot oil, and enjoy it with one of the suggested dips and a side dish of your choice.

Quick Recipes

Satay Skewers

SERVES 4:

➤ **2 cloves garlic** | **2 tbs tamarind sauce
(may substitute 1 tsp lemon juice)** |
4 tbs sweet soy sauce | **2 tsp sambal
oelek (Asian market)** | **14 oz chicken
breast fillet** | **16 small wooden skewers**

1 | Peel and crush garlic and mix
with tamarind sauce, soy sauce, and
sambal oelek.

2 | Cut chicken breast fillet into cubes of
about $1/3$ inch and pierce with skewers.
Marinate with the sauce in the refrigerator
for several hours.

Sesame Chicken

SERVES 4:

➤ **2 tbs flour** | **Salt and pepper** | **Ground
coriander** | **1 egg** | **$1/2$ cup sesame
seeds** | **$10^{1}/_{2}$ oz chicken breast fillet**

1 | Combine flour, salt, pepper, and
coriander on a plate. On a second plate,
whisk egg. On a third plate, sprinkle
sesame seeds.

2 | Cut meat into bite-size cubes and, a
few at a time, roll first in flour, then in the
egg, and finally in the sesame seeds. This
dish goes with Garlic Mascarpone Sauce
(see page 41).

For Gourmets | Asian

Wrapped Shrimp

SERVES 4:

- ➤ 16 peeled, cooked jumbo shrimp
- 1 small clove garlic
- 2 tbs light soy sauce
- 1 tbs tamarind sauce (may substitute 1 tsp lemon juice)
- 1/2 tsp sambal manis (Asian market)
- 16 frozen wonton skins
- 1 tsp cornstarch

🕓 Prep time: 30 minutes
🕓 Marinating time: 1 hour
➤ Calories per serving: About 155

1 | Rinse shrimp under cold water and pat dry. If necessary, slit down the backs and remove dark veins.

2 | Peel garlic and crush in a bowl. Stir in soy sauce, tamarind sauce, and sambal manis. Add shrimp, cover, and marinate in the refrigerator for 1 hour. In the meantime, thaw wonton skins under a kitchen towel. Refreeze any skins you don't use.

3 | Stir cornstarch into a little cold water until smooth. Lay out wonton skins on a cutting board a few at a time, brush edges with cornstarch mixture, and wrap one marinated shrimp in each. Arrange on a platter.

Asian | For Gourmets

Crispy Spring Rolls

SERVES 4:

- ➤ 2 dried shiitake mushrooms
- 1 piece fresh ginger (hazelnut-size)
- 1 clove garlic
- 1 chili pepper
- 2 tbs soy sauce
- Black pepper
- 3 1/2 oz chicken breast fillet
- 25 frozen wonton skins
- 2 oz fresh mung bean sprouts
- 1 tsp oil

🕓 Prep time: 40 minutes
🕓 Marinating time: 1 hour
➤ Calories per serving: About 120

1 | Soak mushrooms in warm water for 20 minutes. Peel garlic and ginger. Clean and rinse chili pepper. Dice these last three ingredients finely and combine with soy sauce and black pepper.

2 | Cut up meat very finely or dice. Toss with marinade, cover, and marinate for at least 1 hour. Cover wonton skins and let thaw.

3 | Rinse bean sprouts, drain, and cut into slightly smaller pieces. Drain mushrooms, remove hard stems, and dice finely.

4 | In a pan, heat oil and brown mushrooms, bean sprouts, and chicken with marinade for 1 minute while stirring. Transfer to a bowl and let cool slightly.

5 | Remove individual wonton skins from the stack. Brush edges with a little cold water and place 1 tsp chicken mixture on the pastry. Fold two opposite corners toward the middle over the filling. Start rolling up pastry from one of the other corners. When you reach the end, press together tightly. Arrange all rolls on a platter.

Photo left: **Wrapped Shrimp**   *Photo right:* **Crispy Spring Rolls** ➤

Traditional with a Twist
Saltimbocca Veal Rolls

SERVES 4:

- 12 oz piece of veal (e.g., cutlet meat)
  2 tbs lemon juice
  Salt and pepper
  2 slices prosciutto
  16 small sage leaves
  16 small wooden skewers

🕐 Prep time: 20 minutes

- Calories per serving: About 110

1 | Cut meat into 16 small, paper-thin slices and pound flat. Season with lemon juice, salt, and pepper. Cut ham slices into eighths and place on top.

2 | Rinse sage leaves, dry, and place one leaf on each piece of ham. Roll up little cutlets and secure with wooden skewers.

TIP Turkey or chicken rolls are also delicious. Oil turns the rolls crispy but they're just as good cooked in stock.

Spicy | Can Prepare in Advance
Spicy Chicken Wings

SERVES 4:

- 16 chicken wings (about $2^1/_2$ lb)
  2 cloves garlic
  4 tbs olive oil
  $^1/_2$ tsp dried, crushed chili pepper
  1 tsp dried thyme
  Pepper

🕐 Prep time: 20 minutes

🕐 Marinating time: 3 hours

- Calories per serving: About 310

1 | Using poultry shears, cut apart chicken at the joints. Peel garlic and crush. Combine garlic with oil, crushed chili pepper, thyme, and pepper.

2 | Toss chicken wings with sauce, cover, and marinate in the refrigerator for 3 hours.

TIP The oil has to be very hot to make the chicken wings crispy. Despite the large amounts, this recipe makes only enough to supplement an oil fondue (see page 7) for 4 people.

Can Prepare in Advance
Fiery Spareribs

SERVES 4:

- $2^1/_4$ lb spareribs
  2 cloves garlic
  1 piece fresh ginger (walnut-size)
  6 tbs soy sauce
  2 tbs maple syrup
  $^1/_2$ tsp dried, crushed chili pepper

🕐 Prep time: 20 minutes

🕐 Marinating time: 3 hours

- Calories per serving: About 205

1 | Cut up spareribs into individual ribs and cut these crosswise into pieces the length of a finger.

2 | Peel garlic and ginger and chop very finely. In a large bowl, combine garlic, ginger, soy sauce, maple syrup, and crushed chili pepper. Add ribs, toss well with sauce, cover, and marinate in the refrigerator for at least 3 hours.

Easy | Hearty

Colorful Turkey Skewers

SERVES 4:

- **9 oz turkey breast fillet**
  Salt and pepper
  Hungarian sweet paprika
  12 dried apricots
  (about 2$\frac{1}{2}$ oz)
  6 thin slices bacon
  (about 2$\frac{1}{2}$ oz)
  2 small zucchini
  (about 7 oz)
  24 wooden skewers

- ⏱ Prep time: 45 minutes
- Calories per serving: About 230

1 | Cut turkey breast fillet into cubes of about $\frac{1}{2}$ inch and season generously with salt, pepper, and paprika.

2 | Rinse apricots under hot water and dry. Cut bacon slices in half and wrap around apricots. Cut wrapped apricots in half. Rinse zucchini, trim, cut in half lengthwise, and cut crosswise into slices of about $\frac{1}{2}$ inch.

3 | Place 1 zucchini slice, $\frac{1}{2}$ wrapped apricot, and 1 cube meat on each wooden skewer and decoratively arrange skewers on a platter.

- ➤ Variations: For liver skewers, cut calf's liver into cubes of about $\frac{1}{2}$ inch, season, and place on skewers with onion pieces and apple wedges.

  For sausage skewers, thread skewers with small pieces of sausage, diced bell pepper, and green onion pieces.

Inexpensive | Vegetarian

Battered Vegetables

SERVES 4:

- **2$\frac{1}{4}$ lb mixed vegetables**
  (e.g., cauliflower, broccoli, zucchini, eggplant, sugar snap peas, bell peppers, mushrooms)
  1 bunch parsley
  4 eggs
  1$\frac{1}{2}$ cups plus 1 tbs flour
  $\frac{3}{4}$ cup red wine
  (may substitute strong vegetable stock)
  Salt and pepper
  Hungarian sweet paprika

- ⏱ Prep time: 20 minutes
- Calories per serving: About 320

1 | Rinse and trim vegetables. Cut all vegetables into bite-size pieces (florets, cubes, or slices). Pat dry with paper towels and arrange on platters or plates.

2 | Rinse parsley, shake dry, and chop leaves finely. In a bowl, stir together parsley, eggs, flour, and red wine to form a thick batter. Season generously with salt, pepper, and paprika.

3 | Pour batter into individual bowls and place on the table along with vegetables. Spear vegetables with a fondue fork, dip in batter, let excess drip off, hold in the hot fat, and cook.

- ➤ Variation: You can also coat fish and seafood well with batter and deep-fry it, or simply dust it with flour and dip it in the hot oil.

Photo left: **Colorful Turkey Skewers**   *Photo right:* **Battered Vegetables** ➤

Low-Fat Stock Fondue

Delicious light dining! Low-calorie fun! All this is made possible by taking a culinary trip to Asia where fondue has always been prepared with stock (see pages 10–11). It's wonderfully light, with meat, fish, and lots of vegetables accompanied by tangy sauces and dips—perfect for anyone who enjoys experimenting and finds the traditional oil fondue too heavy and rich. The recipe ideas in this chapter can be cooked in hot stock in any fondue pot or a traditional Mongolian hot pot (see page 17). Choose your favorites.

Quick Recipes

Vegetable Dumplings

SERVES 4:

➤ 7 oz cauliflower or broccoli florets |
Salt | 2 eggs | 1¼ cup bread crumbs
(approx 2 oz) | 2 tbs semolina |
Freshly grated nutmeg | Pepper

1 | Cover cauliflower or broccoli florets
with a little salted water and cook for
just under 10 minutes. Remove, drain,
and purée.

2 | Stir together eggs, bread crumbs, and
semolina and season with salt, nutmeg,
and pepper. Let stand for 10 minutes and
then shape into 25 walnut-size balls or
dumplings. Arrange on a plate. Serve with
Herbed Ricotta Cream (see page 45).

Zucchini Rolls

SERVES 4:

➤ 2 zucchini | 2 tsp chopped dill |
Pepper | 2 slices cooked ham |
16 small wooden skewers

1 | Cut zucchini in half crosswise and cut
halves into thin slices lengthwise using
either a mandoline or a knife. Season
with dill and pepper.

2 | Cut ham into 16 small pieces, place on
top of zucchini slices, and roll up carefully.
Secure with wooden skewers and arrange
on a plate.

Can Prepare in Advance
Soy-Marinated Pork Fillet

SERVES 4:

➤ 1 piece fresh ginger (about walnut-size)

2 cloves garlic

2 tbs soy sauce

2 tbs oyster sauce

2 tsp rice vinegar

1 tsp sesame oil

Black pepper

10$^1/_2$ oz pork fillet

1 handful cilantro

🕐 Prep time: 20 minutes

🕐 Marinating time: 2 hours

➤ Calories per serving: About 100

1 | Peel ginger and garlic, dice very finely, and combine with soy sauce, oyster sauce, vinegar, sesame oil, and pepper.

2 | Cut meat into paper-thin slices, toss with marinade, cover, and marinate in the refrigerator for 2 hours. Arrange on a platter for serving. Rinse cilantro, shake dry, chop leaves coarsely, and sprinkle over the top.

Mediterranean | Low-Cal
Turkey Meatballs

SERVES 4:

➤ 10$^1/_2$ oz turkey breast fillet

$^1/_2$ bunch parsley

1 egg

1 egg yolk

1 tsp lemon peel from 1 lemon

3 tbs ground almonds

2 tbs chopped almonds

Salt and pepper

🕐 Prep time: 20 minutes

➤ Calories per serving: About 195

1 | Remove skin and sinews from turkey meat and process with the fine cutting disk of a meat grinder or chop finely in a blender or food processor.

2 | Rinse parsley, shake dry, and chop leaves. Combine with egg, egg yolk, lemon peel, almonds, salt, pepper, and meat.

3 | Mix all these ingredients thoroughly, season generously, and shape into walnut-size balls. Cover and refrigerate until ready to serve.

Impressive
Asparagus Wrapped in Spinach

SERVES 4:

➤ 1 lb white asparagus

Salt

7 oz spinach leaves

2 slices cooked ham

Freshly grated nutmeg

🕐 Prep time: 30 minutes

➤ Calories per serving: About 75

1 | Rinse asparagus, snap off tough ends, peel bottom, and cut into pieces the length of a finger. Bring 1 quart salted water to a boil and, depending on its thickness, precook asparagus for 4–8 minutes until al dente. Pour into a colander, rinse in ice-cold water, and drain.

2 | Rinse and sort spinach. Pour boiling water over the top, immediately transfer to a colander, rinse in ice-cold water, and drain.

3 | Cut ham into short pieces about 2 inches wide. Season asparagus with nutmeg, then carefully wrap it in ham and spinach. Arrange decoratively on a platter.

Fast | Low-Fat

Hearty Fish Skewers

SERVES 4:

➤ 14 oz firm fish fillet (e.g., cod)

2 tbs lemon juice

1 tbs green Tabasco (may substitute red Tabasco)

Salt and pepper

2 fat garlic cloves

10–12 small cherry tomatoes (approx $3^1/_2$ oz)

16 small wooden skewers

🕑 Prep time: 25 minutes

➤ Calories per serving: About 80

1 | Cut fish fillet into cubes of about $^1/_2$ inch. Combine lemon juice, Tabasco, salt, and pepper and toss with fish cubes.

2 | Peel garlic and slice but not too thinly. Rinse and dry cherry tomatoes.

3 | Alternate ingredients on wooden skewers and arrange decoratively on a plate to serve.

➤ Variations: For colorful shrimp skewers, season 9 oz large shrimp, and thread onto skewers along with small bell pepper pieces and garlic slices, if desired. For seafood skewers, thread skewers with peeled shrimp, pieces of cleaned octopus, mussels removed from the shells, and zucchini slices and season with cayenne pepper or Tabasco.

Low-Cal | Impressive

Caribbean Fish Rolls

SERVES 4:

➤ $10^1/_2$ oz sole or flounder fillets

4 tbs lime juice

2 tbs chili sauce

1 tbs tamarind sauce (may substitute lemon juice)

Salt

White pepper

$^1/_2$ tsp cumin

$^1/_2$ ripe avocado

🕑 Prep time: 40 minutes

➤ Calories per serving: About 135

1 | Rinse fish under cold water, pat dry, and cut into strips $^3/_4$ inch–$1^1/_4$ inch wide. Spread out on a large board and drizzle with 2 tbs lime juice.

2 | Combine chili sauce, tamarind sauce, salt, pepper, and cumin and brush onto fish strips.

3 | Peel avocado half, cut into thick slices, and cut slices into strips. Drizzle immediately with remaining lime juice and season with salt and pepper. Lay 1 avocado piece across each fish strip.

4 | Roll fish strips around avocado pieces and secure with wooden skewers.

➤ Variation: Instead of avocado, try some tropical fruit fillings. Wrap the fish around strips of pineapple, papaya, mango, or banana.

Photo top: **Hearty Fish Skewers**   *Photo bottom:* **Caribbean Fish Rolls** ➤

Asian | Low-Cal
Vietnamese Rice Paper Rolls

SERVES 4:

- 1 small clove garlic
- 1 small red chili pepper
- 2 tbs fish sauce (Asian market)
- 4½ oz chicken breast fillet
- 2 oz glass noodles
- 2 oz mung bean sprouts
- 1 carrot
- 2 sprigs mint
- 1 tsp soy oil
- 16 round rice paper wrappers (5 inches diameter; Asian market)

⏱ Prep time: 40 minutes
➤ Calories per serving: About 135

1 | Peel garlic. Rinse chili pepper, cut in half, and clean. Chop both ingredients finely and stir into fish sauce. Cut chicken breast fillet into thin strips and toss with marinade.

2 | Place glass noodles in a bowl, pour hot water over the top, and soak for 15 minutes.

3 | Rinse bean sprouts under cold water and drain. Peel carrot and grate coarsely. Rinse mint, shake dry, and chop leaves.

4 | In a nonstick pan, heat oil and sauté chicken on all sides for 2 minutes. Remove and combine with other prepared ingredients.

5 | Soak rice paper wrappers one at a time and for several minutes in cold water. Lay out on a board. Place 1 tbs filling in the center of each and wrap up carefully.

TIPS

➤ These rolls are a sophisticated supplement to a Mongolian hot pot. Side dishes are described on page 17.

➤ In an Asian market, you'll find dried rice paper wrappers of various shapes and sizes. If you've never used them before, use 2 wrappers for each roll.

1 Marinate
Toss thin strips of meat with marinade.

2 Mix
Mix browned meat with other ingredients.

3 Fill
After soaking rice paper wrappers, place 1 tbs filling on each.

4 Roll
Fold in sides of rice paper before rolling.

39

Essential Sauces and Dips

What makes fondue such a culinary treat are the accompanying sauces and dips. You should provide four to six different sauces to encourage your guests to dip and experiment. Choose your own favorites from the suggestions in this chapter. All of the sauces go with almost any oil fondue, stock fondue, or hot pot. For ideas on possible combinations, see pages 58 and 59.

Quick Recipes

Garlic-Mascarpone Sauce

SERVES 4:

➤ 4 cloves garlic | ³/₄ cup mascarpone |
2 tbs sour cream | Salt and pepper |
1 tbs olive oil | ¹/₂ bunch garlic chives
(may substitute chives)

1 | Peel garlic. Finely chop 2 cloves and
combine with mascarpone and sour cream.
Season to taste with salt and pepper.

2 | Thinly slice remaining garlic. Heat
oil and sauté garlic until golden brown.
Stir into mascarpone mixture. Rinse
garlic chives, shake dry, chop, and
sprinkle on top.

Hot-Sweet Tomato Dip

SERVES 4:

➤ 6 tbs tomato paste | 6 tbs fruit vinegar |
¹/₂ cup sugar | ¹/₂ tsp dried, crushed
chili pepper | Salt and pepper |
1 tsp chopped chives

1 | In a small pot over low heat, bring to
a boil tomato paste, vinegar, sugar, and
crushed chili pepper while stirring.

2 | Season dip to taste with salt and
pepper. Transfer to a small bowl and
let cool. Sprinkle with chives.

Asian | Hearty
Spicy Peanut Sauce

SERVES 4:

➤ 2 small red chili peppers
 2 small cloves garlic
 2 shallots
 $1/3$ cup (heaping) unsalted roasted peanuts (approx 2 oz)
 2 tbs sweet soy sauce
 $1/3$ cup vegetable stock
 1 handful cilantro leaves

🕓 Prep time: 10 minutes
➤ Calories per serving: About 100

1 | Slit open chili peppers, remove seeds, trim, and rinse. Peel garlic and shallots. Purée all these ingredients along with peanuts, soy sauce, and stock to form a thick sauce.

2 | Transfer sauce to a small bowl. Rinse cilantro, shake dry, chop leaves coarsely, and sprinkle over sauce.

TIP

This sauce is a traditional accompaniment to Indonesian Satay Skewers (recipe on page 25) but also goes well with other fondue creations.

Mediterranean | Inexpensive
Tomato-White Bean Dip

SERVES 4:

➤ 1 (15-oz) can white beans
 1 small onion
 4 tsp olive oil
 1 clove garlic
 Salt and pepper
 4 tsp balsamic vinegar
 5 dried tomatoes in oil
 4 sprigs basil

🕓 Prep time: 20 minutes
➤ Calories per serving: About 150

1 | Mash beans and liquid with a potato masher. Peel onion and dice very finely. Heat oil and sauté onion until golden. Peel garlic, squeeze through a press, and add.

2 | Add beans and heat. Season with salt, pepper, and vinegar to taste.

3 | Cut tomatoes into thin strips. Rinse basil, shake dry, and chop leaves. Stir both ingredients into dip.

Inexpensive | Fast
Garbanzo Bean Dip

SERVES 4:

➤ 1 (15-oz) can garbanzo beans
 1 red onion
 1 tbs oil
 1 clove garlic
 $1/2$ tsp cumin
 Salt and pepper
 2 sprigs mint

🕓 Prep time: 15 minutes
➤ Calories per serving: About 170

1 | Purée garbanzo beans with liquid. Peel onion and dice finely.

2 | Heat oil and sauté diced onion until translucent. Peel garlic, squeeze through a press, and add. Stir in puréed garbanzo beans, heat, cover halfway with a lid (it might splatter!), and simmer over low heat for 5 minutes. Season to taste with cumin, salt, and pepper.

3 | Rinse mint, shake dry, chop leaves, and stir into dip.

Inexpensive | Easy

Yogurt-Walnut Dip

SERVES 4:

- ½ bunch each of Italian parsley, chives, and basil
  1 clove garlic
  2 tbs walnuts
  ½ cup low-fat yogurt
  1 tbs walnut oil
  Salt and pepper

- Prep time: 10 minutes
- Calories per serving: About 70

1 | Rinse herbs and shake dry. Chop parsley and basil finely and chop chives. Peel garlic and squeeze through a press. Chop walnuts.

2 | Combine herbs, garlic, walnuts, yogurt, and oil. Season to taste with salt and pepper. Transfer to a small bowl.

Can Prepare in Advance

Herbed Ricotta Cream

SERVES 4:

- 1 bunch basil
  ½ bunch chives
  ½ bunch garlic chives (may substitute 2 green onions)
  1 cup ricotta
  2 dried tomatoes in oil
  Salt and pepper
  1 tbs pine nuts

- Prep time: 15 minutes
- Calories per serving: About 155

1 | Rinse herbs, shake dry, and purée along with ricotta until smooth.

2 | Dice tomatoes very finely and stir into ricotta cream. Season to taste with salt and pepper.

3 | Toast pine nuts in a non-stick pan without oil until golden brown and let cool. Transfer cream to a small bowl and sprinkle with pine nuts.

Fast | Inexpensive

Cranberry-Orange Sauce

SERVES 4:

- 1 orange
  1 cup candied cranberries
  1 tbs sour cream
  1 tbs mayonnaise
  Salt and pepper

- Prep time: 15 minutes
- Calories per serving: About 95

1 | Rinse orange under hot water and dry. Remove a little peel with a zester, cut into thin strips, and finely grate 1 tsp zest from remaining orange. Continue peeling orange so that the white outer membrane is also removed. Cut segments out of the inner membrane, saving any juice.

2 | Combine cranberries, sour cream, mayonnaise, grated orange zest, and the orange juice you saved. Chop orange segments and stir into sauce. Garnish with salt and pepper. Transfer to a small bowl and sprinkle with orange peel strips.

Exotic | Impressive

Caribbean Coconut Dip

SERVES 4:

➤ 1 green onion
1 red chili pepper
1 small clove garlic
1 tsp oil
³/₄ cup canned coconut milk
2 slices pineapple
Salt and pepper

🕐 Prep time: 20 minutes
➤ Calories per serving: About 35

1 | Rinse green onion and cut into thin, diagonal rings. Slit open chili pepper, remove seeds, trim, and cut into thin strips. Peel and chop garlic.

2 | Heat oil and sauté green onion, chili pepper, and garlic until translucent. Add coconut milk.

3 | Remove peel and core from pineapple, dice very finely, and stir into sauce. Season to taste with salt and pepper. Transfer to a small bowl and let cool.

Exotic | Low-Cal

Cucumber Dip with Ginger

SERVES 4:

➤ 1 onion
1 piece fresh ginger (about walnut-size)
2 cloves garlic
5 oz cucumber (about ¹/₂ medium-size cucumber)
1 tbs oil
1 tsp sambal manis (Asian market; may substitute sambal oelek)
2 tbs soy sauce

🕐 Prep time: 15 minutes
➤ Calories per serving: About 35

1 | Peel onion, ginger, and garlic and chop each very finely. Peel and seed cucumber and grate finely into a bowl.

2 | Heat oil and sauté chopped onion over medium heat until translucent. Add ginger and garlic and brown briefly. Stir in grated cucumber and cucumber juice and simmer briefly over low heat. Season with sambal manis and soy sauce. Transfer dip to a small bowl and let cool.

Exotic | Inexpensive

Curry-Coconut Sauce

SERVES 4:

➤ 1 onion
1 tbs oil
1¹/₂ tsp flour
1 tsp green curry paste (Asian market; may substitute 2 teaspoons curry powder)
¹/₂ cup canned coconut milk
Salt
Several sprigs cilantro

🕐 Prep time: 15 minutes
➤ Calories per serving: About 115

1 | Peel onion and dice finely. Heat oil and sauté onion until translucent. Dust with flour and sauté without browning. Stir in curry paste.

2 | While stirring, add coconut milk. Season sauce with salt and let cool.

3 | Rinse cilantro, shake dry, chop, and sprinkle over sauce.

Mediterranean | Fast
Cheese Sauce

SERVES 4:

➤ 3 oz fontina
(Italian raw-milk cheese)

3 oz Gorgonzola

$1/2$ cup milk

5 tbs dry white wine

Pepper

2 sprigs basil

🕐 Prep time: 10 minutes

➤ Calories per serving:
About 180

1 | Dice fontina finely and Gorgonzola coarsely. In a small pot, bring milk to a boil and stir in cheese over low heat while stirring constantly to melt. Let cool.

2 | Before serving, mix sauce with a hand blender while adding wine. Season to taste with pepper. Rinse basil, shake dry, and use to garnish sauce.

TIP For a spicier sauce, replace the Gorgonzola with a strong Roquefort and add 1–2 tbs pickled green peppercorns.

Mediterranean | Inexpensive
Black Olive Dip

SERVES 4:

➤ 1 (6-oz) can pitted black olives

1 tbs lemon juice

5 tbs olive oil

1 tsp Dijon mustard

2 tbs balsamic vinegar

4 sprigs thyme

Salt and pepper

2 green pimento olives

🕐 Prep time: 10 minutes

➤ Calories per serving:
About 140

1 | Chop olives very finely, then combine with lemon juice, oil, mustard, and vinegar.

2 | Rinse thyme, shake dry, strip off leaves, and stir into dip. Season dip generously with salt and pepper.

3 | Transfer dip to a small bowl. Cut green olives in half and use to garnish dip.

Spicy | Easy
Sweet-and-Sour Peach Sauce

SERVES 4:

➤ 3 shallots

2 fresh peaches
(may substitute canned)

1 tbs oil

1 small clove garlic

2 tbs brown sugar

$1/3$ cup stock

Salt and pepper

$1/8$ tsp dried, crushed chili pepper

2 tbs apple vinegar

🕐 Prep time: 15 minutes

➤ Calories per serving:
About 80

1 | Peel shallots and dice finely. Pour boiling water over peaches, peel, remove pits, and dice finely. Heat oil and sauté shallots until translucent. Peel garlic, squeeze through a press, and add.

2 | Add peaches, sugar, and stock to pan and simmer over low heat for 5 minutes. Season with salt, pepper, crushed chili pepper, and vinegar. Transfer sauce to a small bowl and let cool.

Seductive Side Dishes

These days, every fine meal includes a small baguette or some other kind of bread, and bread should also be part of your fondue dinner. It's even better if you vary the choices. For example, surprise your guests with homemade herb and cheese rolls along with tempting salads that guests can serve themselves at the table.

Quick Recipes

Multicolor Vegetable Salad

SERVES 4:

➤ 2 tender green onions │ 1 kohlrabi │
2 small carrots │ 7 oz cucumber (about
$^1/_2$ large cucumber) │ 1 tart apple │
3 tbs lemon juice │ 3 tbs olive oil │ Salt
and pepper │ $^1/_2$ bunch watercress

1 │ Rinse green onion, kohlrabi, carrots,
cucumber, and apple and cut into thin
rings, small cubes, or thin slices.

2 │ Whisk together lemon juice, oil, salt,
and pepper and stir in cut-up vegetables
and apples. Rinse watercress, remove
tough stems, and stir into salad.

Salmon-Cucumber Tartare

SERVES 4:

➤ 1 tart apple │ 6 oz cucumber (about
$^1/_2$ medium-size cucumber) │ 4 oz
smoked salmon │ 1 tbs lemon juice │
Salt and pepper │ $^1/_4$ tsp ground
coriander │ $^1/_2$ bunch dill

1 │ Rinse apple, cut into quarters, and
remove core. Peel cucumber and remove
seeds. Dice apple, cucumber, and salmon
very finely.

2 │ In a bowl, combine ingredients
above with lemon juice, salt, pepper,
and coriander. Rinse dill, shake dry,
chop, and sprinkle over salad.

Can Prepare in Advance

Greek Feta Rolls

MAKES 8 ROLLS:

- ➤ 1 (^{1}/$_4$-oz) package active dry yeast
  ^{1}/$_2$ cup lukewarm water
  ^{1}/$_2$ tsp sugar
  1^1/$_2$ cups plus 1 tbs flour
  2 tbs olive oil
  1 tsp salt
  ^{1}/$_2$ tsp dried oregano
  8, ^{3}/$_4$-inch cubes feta
  Baking parchment

- ◷ Prep time: 45 minutes
- ◷ Standing time: 2^1/$_2$ hours
- ◷ Baking time: About 15 minutes
- ➤ Calories per roll: About 95

1 | Stir yeast into a little warm water along with sugar and 1 tbs flour until smooth. Cover and let stand for 15 minutes.

2 | Add remaining flour, remaining warm water, oil, salt, and oregano and knead into a smooth, pliable dough. Cover and let stand in a moderately warm place for 2 hours.

3 | Knead dough vigorously and divide into 8 equal portions. Shape each into a roll with 1 cheese cube in the center.

4 | Place rolls on a baking sheet lined with baking parchment, cover, and let stand for 15 minutes.

5 | Preheat oven to 400°F. Bake rolls in the hot oven (middle rack) for 12–15 minutes until golden.

For Gourmets | Inexpensive

Hearty Mini Muffins

MAKES 12 MUFFINS:

- ➤ 1 cup plus 2 tsp flour
  2 tsp baking powder
  Salt and pepper
  1 oz freshly grated Parmesan
  ^{1}/$_3$ cup dried tomatoes in oil
  ^{1}/$_2$ bunch basil
  1 egg
  3 tbs olive oil
  ^{1}/$_3$ cup low-fat yogurt
  Oil for greasing tin

- ◷ Prep time: 20 minutes
- ◷ Baking time: About 30 minutes
- ➤ Calories per muffin: About 90

1 | Preheat oven to 400°F. Brush oil into the cups of a muffin tin for 12 mini muffins.

2 | Combine flour, baking powder, ^{1}/$_4$ tsp salt, ^{1}/$_4$ tsp pepper, and Parmesan. Dice tomatoes finely and add. Rinse basil, shake dry, chop leaves, and add. Stir mixture together.

3 | Add egg, oil, and yogurt and stir to obtain a smooth batter. Pour batter into the cups of the greased muffin tin.

4 | Bake muffins in the oven (middle rack) for about 30 minutes until golden brown. Best when served lukewarm.

Mediterranean | Fast
Arugula-Carrot Salad

SERVES 4:

➤ **2 tbs pine nuts**
4 oz arugula
2 small carrots
3^1/$_2$ oz Swiss cheese
1 onion
3 tbs balsamic vinegar
Salt and black pepper
6 tbs olive oil
**2 sprigs lemon thyme
(may substitute thyme)**

🕐 Prep time: 25 minutes
➤ Calories per serving:
About 290

1 | In a nonstick pan, toast pine nuts without oil until golden brown. Remove and set aside.

2 | Rinse arugula, sort, and shake dry. If necessary, tear into bite-size pieces. Peel carrots and grate coarsely or slice. Cut cheese into fine strips.

3 | Peel onion and dice very finely. Whisk together with vinegar, salt, and pepper. Beat in oil and season dressing to taste.

4 | Toss arugula, carrots, and cheese with dressing. Sprinkle with pine nuts. Rinse thyme, shake dry, strip off leaves, and sprinkle over salad.

Can Prepare in Advance
Herb Cheese Rolls

MAKES 8 ROLLS:

➤ **1 (^{1}/$_4$-oz) package active dry yeast**
1 cup lukewarm water
^{1}/$_2$ tsp sugar
2^1/$_3$ cups flour
3 tbs olive oil
2 tsp dried thyme
1^1/$_2$ teaspoons salt
Flour for working dough
1 egg yolk for brushing on
1 oz grated Swiss cheese for sprinkling
Baking parchment

🕐 Prep time: 1 hour
🕐 Standing time: 1 hour
🕐 Baking time: About 20 minutes
➤ Calories per roll: About 195

1 | Stir yeast into a little warm water along with sugar and 1 tbs flour. Cover and let stand for 15 minutes.

2 | Add remaining warm water, flour, oil, thyme, and salt and knead into a pliable dough. Cover and let stand in a warm place for 30 minutes.

3 | Knead dough once more on a lightly floured surface. Divide into 8 equal portions, roll out into long sticks the thickness of a finger, and roll up into snails. Place on a baking sheet lined with baking parchment, cover, and let stand for another 15 minutes.

4 | Preheat oven to 400°F. Whisk egg yolk and brush onto rolls. Sprinkle with cheese. Bake in the oven (middle rack) for 15–20 minutes until golden brown and let cool on a rack.

➤ Variation: For bacon rolls, dice 3^1/$_2$ oz bacon very finely, fry in a pan until crispy, let cool, and knead into dough after the first rising period. Otherwise preparation is the same.

Photo top: **Arugula-Carrot Salad**   *Photo bottom:* **Herb Cheese Rolls** ➤

Can Prepare in Advance
Yellow and Green Potato Salad

SERVES 4:

- 1 1/3 lb small, firm potatoes
  1 bunch chives
  1 bunch Italian parsley
  Salt and pepper
  3 tbs white wine vinegar
  3 tbs olive oil
  2 tbs walnut oil
  1 (15 1/4-oz) can corn kernels
  4 tbs walnuts

🕐 Prep time: 45 minutes
- Calories per serving: About 600

1 | Cook unpeeled potatoes in water for 25 minutes until done. Let cool slightly, peel, and slice.

2 | Rinse herbs, shake dry, and chop. Combine with salt, pepper, and vinegar and beat in both types of oil.

3 | Drain corn and toss with dressing. Carefully add potatoes and season with salt and pepper. Chop nuts and sprinkle on top.

Exotic | Easy
Colorful Sprout Salad

SERVES 4:

- 4 shallots
  1 piece fresh ginger (about walnut-size)
  2 tbs rice vinegar
  Salt and pepper
  6 tbs oil
  7 oz white radish
  1 carrot
  5 oz cucumbers (about 1/2 medium-size cucumber)
  5 oz mixed sprouts
  3 tbs cashews

🕐 Prep time: 30 minutes
- Calories per serving: About 235

1 | Peel shallots and ginger and chop very finely. Whisk together with vinegar, salt, and pepper. Beat in oil and season dressing generously to taste.

2 | Trim radish, carrot, and cucumber, peel, and grate each coarsely. Rinse sprouts briefly, shake dry, and tear into smaller pieces. Toss vegetables with dressing.

3 | Chop cashews coarsely, toast briefly in a pan, and sprinkle over salad.

Fruity | Mediterranean
Spinach Salad with Grapefruit

SERVES 4:

- 2 pink grapefruit
  4 oz spinach leaves
  2 red onions
  2 tsp chopped chives
  1 tsp thyme leaves
  3 tbs red wine vinegar
  Salt and pepper
  6 tbs olive oil
  2 oz black olives

🕐 Prep time: 30 minutes
- Calories per serving: About 180

1 | Peel grapefruit, including white membrane. Cut segments out of the inner membrane, saving any juice.

2 | Rinse spinach, sort, and break off coarse stems. Peel onions, cut in half, and then into fine strips.

3 | Whisk together herbs, vinegar, salt, pepper, a little grapefruit juice, and oil. Toss with grapefruit segments, spinach, and onions. Remove pits from olives, chop coarsely, and sprinkle over the top.

◀ *Photo top:* **Yellow and Green Potato Salad**　　*Photo middle:* **Colorful Sprout Salad**
Photo bottom: **Spinach Salad with Grapefruit**

57

Ideas for Fondue Nights

Classic for 4

1. **Prepare:** Fondue Bourguignonne (page 13)
2. **Serve with:** Garlic-Mascarpone Sauce (page 41), Cranberry-Orange Sauce (page 45), Cheese Sauce (page 49), Tomato-White Bean Dip (page 43); Yellow and Green Potato Salad (page 57), baguette, gherkins, cocktail onions, marinated vegetables
3. **Beverages:** Mineral water, dry red wine

Cheese Fondue for 4

1. **Prepare:** Swiss Cheese Fondue (page 21)
2. **Serve with:** Mixed pickles
3. **Beverages:** Mineral water, tea, and dry white wine

Cheese Fondue for 6

1. **Prepare:** Rustic Fondue (page 13), 1½ x recipe
2. **Serve with:** Multicolor Vegetable Salad (page 51), marinated baby corn, small mushrooms, pear and apple wedges, blanched broccoli and cauliflower florets
3. **Beverages:** Mineral water, tea, dry white wine

Chinese Night for 4

1. **Prepare:** Mongolian Hot Pot (page 17)
2. **Serve with:** Hot-Sweet Tomato Dip (page 41), Cucumber Dip with Ginger (page 47), Spicy Peanut Sauce (page 43), Sweet-and-Sour Peach Sauce (page 49); Colorful Sprout Salad (page 57), cooked aromatic rice (e.g., jasmine), soy sauce, chili sauce, candied ginger
3. **Beverages:** Mineral water, green tea, cold Asian beer (such as TsingTao)

Low-Fat Fondue for 6

1. **Prepare:** Stock (page 10, 11); Vegetable Dumplings (page 33), Soy-Marinated Pork Fillet (page 35), Hearty Fish Skewers (page 36), Asparagus Wrapped in Spinach (page 35)
2. **Serve with:** Yogurt-Walnut Dip (page 45), Cucumber Dip with Ginger (page 47), Garbanzo Bean Dip (page 43), Herbed Ricotta Cream (page 45); presoaked rice noodles, Multicolor Vegetable Salad (page 51)
3. **Beverages:** Mineral water, dry white wine

Large Fondue for 8

1. **Prepare:** 2 stock fondue pots (page 10); 1 lb thinly sliced beef filet, Zucchini Rolls (page 33), Turkey Meatballs (page 35), Asparagus Wrapped in Spinach (page 35)
2. **Serve with:** 1½ x each of the following recipes: Garlic-Mascarpone Sauce (page 41), Black Olive Dip (page 49), Cheese Sauce (page 49), Carribean Coconut Dip (page 47); bread, rice noodles, potato salad (double recipe)
3. **Beverages:** Mineral water, white wine

Cheese Fondue for 6

1. **Prepare:** Cheese Fondue (page 8), 1½ x recipe, seasoned with chopped dill
2. **Serve with:** Salmon-Cucumber Tartare (double recipe, page 51), peeled cooked shrimp, small boiled potatoes, blanched broccoli florets
3. **Beverages:** Mineral water, tea, and dry white wine, if desired

Fish Fondue for 6

1. **Prepare:** Stock (page 10, 11), 1⅓ lb mixed fish fillet, diced; Hearty Fish Skewers (page 36), Caribbean Fish Rolls (page 36)
2. **Serve with:** Herbed Ricotta Cream (page 45), Yogurt-Walnut Dip (page 45), Caribbean Coconut Dip (page 47), Curry Coconut Sauce (page 47); Salmon-Cucumber Tartare (page 51), Herb Cheese Rolls (page 54); baguette
3. **Beverages:** Mineral water, dry white wine

Asian Fondue for 2

1. **Prepare:** Mixed Meat and Vegetable fondue with 9 oz meat (page 15), Wrapped Shrimp (page 26), ½ x recipe ; Satay Skewers (page 25), ½ x recipe
2. **Serve with:** Spicy Peanut Sauce (page 43), Curry-Coconut Sauce (page 47), Cucumber Dip with Ginger (page 47), Colorful Sprout Salad (page 57), ½ x recipe; baguette
3. **Beverages:** Green tea, white wine

Fast Fondue for 4

1. **Prepare:** Fondue Bourguignonne with 14 oz meat (page 13); Battered Vegetables (page 30)
2. **Serve with:** Garlic-Mascarpone Sauce (page 41), Yogurt-Walnut Dip (page 45); 2 store-bought prepared sauces, various store-bought mini rolls; Arugula-Carrot Salad (page 54)
3. **Beverages:** Mineral water, dry white wine

Vegetarian Fondue for 4

1. **Prepare:** Stock (page 10, 11)
2. **Plus:** 5 oz bean sprouts, 7 oz small mushrooms, 1 bell pepper, 10 oz zucchini, 2 leeks
3. **Serve with:** Vegetable Dumplings (page 33), Spicy Peanut Sauce (page 43), Herbed Ricotta Cream (page 45), Black Olive Dip (page 49), Curry-Coconut Sauce (page 47), Yellow and Green Potato Salad (page 57); rustic bread
4. **Beverages:** Mineral water, white wine

Game Fondue for 4

1. **Prepare:** Sauté diced onion in fondue pot until translucent, heat with red wine, and season; 1¾ lb tender sliced game meat
2. **Serve with:** Cheese Sauce (page 49), Black Olive Dip (page 49), Garlic-Mascarpone Sauce (page 41), Cranberry-Orange Sauce (page 45); Spinach Salad with Grapefruit (page 57); mini rolls
3. **Beverages:** Mineral water, dry red wine

59

ABBREVIATIONS

approx = approximately
lb = pound
oz = ounce
tsp = teaspoon
tbs = tablespoon

The Author

Angelika Ilies was born in Hamburg, Germany, and now lives near Frankfurt. Immediately after completing her degree in food science, she began her career as a food journalist. After working in the editorial department of a well-known publisher in London, she returned to Germany where she took a position in the culinary department of the largest German food magazine. She has been a successful freelance author and food journalist since 1989.

The Photographer

Jörn Rynio works as a photographer in Hamburg, Germany. His customers include national and international magazines, book publishers and ad agencies. All the recipe photos in this book were produced in his studio with the energetic support of his food stylist, Martina Mehldau.

Photo Credits

All photos: Jörn Rynio, Hamburg

Published originally under the title Fondues: fürs gesellige Vergnügen © 2002 Gräfe und Unzer Verlag GmbH, Munich. English translation for the U.S. market © 2002, Silverback Books, Inc.

Managing editor: Birgit Rademacker
Editor: Elizabeth Penn and Tanja Dusy
Reader: Ann Beman and Redaktionsbüro Maryna Zimdars, Munich
Layout, typography and cover design: Independent Medien Design, Munich
Production: Patty Holden and Maike Harmeier
Typesetting: Patty Holden and Design-Typo-Print, Ismaning

Printed in Singapore

ISBN:1-930603-57-6

Enjoy Other Quick & Easy Books

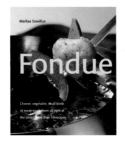

Marlisa Szwillus

Fondue

Cheese, vegetable, th all kinds of meat—cook them all right at the table. More than 50 recipes

Cornelia Adam

Salads

An array of salads to eat as appetizers, entrees, and party dishes. Includes classic choices and cutting-edge alternatives.

Sandwiches

Something new and something new. A variety of breads, garnishes, and fillings

Xenia Burgtorf

Cornelia Adam

Quiche

Delicious, savory pies with vegetables, meat, poultry or fish- serve for all occasions

Cornelia Adam

Garlic

Sophisticated Recipes with this Essential Spice of the Mediterranean Region Spicy (tangy), Fine (delicate), International

Cornelia Schinharl

Easy Vegetarian

Uncomplicated and sophisticated Vegetarian recipes for all seasons

Sebastian Dickhaut

Casseroles

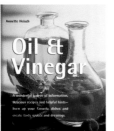

Annette Heisch

Oil & Vinegar

A wonderful source of information, delicious recipes and helpful hints— liven up your favorite dishes and create tasty sauces and dressings.

Andreas Fürtmayr

Sushi

Classic ideas from Japan and new fusion sushi
Home-made perfectly

1 Noodle, 50 Sauces

Everyday Pasta • Old and New Italian Dishes
Noodle biography • 10 Tips for Success

Healthy Wok

Elisabeth Döpp
Christian Willrich
Jörn Rebbe

Great for light and satisfying meals

Antje Gruener

Grilling

Crisp, flavorful and delectable recipes from the grill for that perfect meal, from spareribs to skewered vegetables, with sauces and chutneys.

Gina Greifenstein

1 Batter— 50 Cakes

Baking to your heart's content

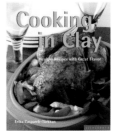

Cooking in Clay

Healthy Recipes with Great Flavor

Erika Casparek-Türkkan

Doris Muliar

Cocktails for Drivers

100% Enjoyment

Antipasti and Tapas

Mediterranean Appetizers
Cornelia Schinharl

Soups

Classic to Contemporary

Sebastian Dickhaut

Claudia Schmidt

Raclette

New Recipes with Cheese Primer and Party Dips

NUMBER OF GUESTS

- ➤ One pot can serve up to six guests.
- ➤ Each person must have free access to the pot.
- ➤ Oil and stock fondues cool off when too many ingredients are dipped into them at once so always take breaks.
- ➤ For parties involving eight or ten guests, borrow a second pot.

Guaranteed Fondue Fun

KNIFE & FORK

- ➤ For each guest, provide a (fondue) plate, knife, fork, and a long-handled fondue fork.
- ➤ With a hot pot, impress your guests by offering rice bowls, chopsticks, and special wire ladles.

DRINKING PLEASURE

- ➤ There are no strict rules regarding wine.
- ➤ Dry chilled wine is best.
- ➤ Serve white or red, as desired. White wine should be served at a temperature of 50–53°F and red wine at about 60°F.

QUANTITIES

- ➤ Experience has shown that 5 to 9 oz meat or fish are required per person.
- ➤ You'll need less if you also offer a wide selection of vegetables and/or fruit.
- ➤ Bread and at least 4 dips are essential; a wider variety is even better.